50 From Home to Tokyo Recipes

By: Kelly Johnson

Table of Contents

- Teriyaki Chicken Skewers
- Homemade Ramen Bowl
- Spicy Tuna Sushi Rolls
- Matcha Green Tea Ice Cream
- Classic Miso Soup
- Pork Tonkatsu with Cabbage
- Shrimp Tempura
- Japanese Curry Rice
- Yakitori Chicken Sticks
- Okonomiyaki Savory Pancakes
- Takoyaki Octopus Balls
- Salmon Onigiri (Rice Balls)
- Udon Noodle Stir-Fry
- Mochi Desserts
- Japanese Cheesecake
- Wagyu Beef Steaks
- Gyudon Beef Bowl
- Edamame with Sea Salt
- Soy Glazed Eggplant
- Gyoza Dumplings
- Katsu Sando (Cutlet Sandwich)
- Cold Soba Noodle Salad
- Tamago Sushi (Egg Sushi)
- Yakiniku Grilled Meats
- Hokkaido Butter Corn Ramen
- Green Tea Mochi Cake
- Sweet Soy Dango Skewers
- Tempura Zaru Soba
- Sashimi Salad
- Japanese Pickles (Tsukemono)
- Shabu-Shabu Hot Pot
- Chicken Karaage (Japanese Fried Chicken)
- Seaweed Salad
- Chawanmushi (Savory Egg Custard)
- Japanese Fried Rice (Chahan)

- Mackerel Sushi (Saba)
- Spicy Mayo Shrimp Rolls
- Matcha Latte
- Eel Donburi (Unadon)
- Japanese Potato Salad
- Tuna Tataki
- Kabocha Tempura
- Japanese Sweet Red Bean Soup (Zenzai)
- Sukiyaki Beef Hotpot
- Yuzu Sorbet
- Japanese Street Crepes
- Nikujaga (Meat and Potato Stew)
- Shio Ramen
- Chirashi Sushi Bowl
- Daifuku Mochi with Strawberry

Teriyaki Chicken Skewers

Ingredients:

- 1 lb chicken breast or thighs, cut into bite-sized pieces
- 1/4 cup soy sauce
- 2 tbsp mirin
- 2 tbsp brown sugar
- 1 tbsp honey
- 1 tsp grated ginger
- 2 cloves garlic, minced
- 1 tbsp sesame oil
- Wooden skewers, soaked in water

Instructions:

1. In a bowl, mix soy sauce, mirin, brown sugar, honey, ginger, garlic, and sesame oil.
2. Add the chicken to the marinade, cover, and refrigerate for at least 30 minutes or up to 2 hours.
3. Preheat the grill or broiler to medium-high heat.
4. Thread the chicken onto the skewers.
5. Grill the skewers for 8-10 minutes, turning and basting with the remaining marinade until the chicken is cooked through and slightly charred.
6. Serve with steamed rice and garnish with sesame seeds and green onions.

Homemade Ramen Bowl

Ingredients:

- 4 cups chicken or pork broth
- 2 tbsp soy sauce
- 1 tbsp miso paste
- 1 tbsp sesame oil
- 2 cloves garlic, minced
- 1 tsp grated ginger
- 2 packs fresh or dried ramen noodles
- Toppings: boiled egg, sliced green onions, nori sheets, sliced cooked pork, corn, bamboo shoots, etc.

Instructions:

1. In a pot, heat sesame oil over medium heat and sauté garlic and ginger until fragrant.
2. Add broth, soy sauce, and miso paste. Simmer for 10 minutes.
3. Cook ramen noodles according to package instructions and divide into bowls.
4. Pour the broth over the noodles.
5. Top with boiled egg, sliced pork, and desired garnishes. Serve hot.

Spicy Tuna Sushi Rolls

Ingredients:

- 1 cup sushi rice, cooked and seasoned with rice vinegar
- 1 sheet nori
- 1/2 cup fresh tuna, diced
- 1 tbsp sriracha
- 1 tsp sesame oil
- 1 tbsp mayonnaise
- Optional: cucumber or avocado slices
- Soy sauce, pickled ginger, and wasabi for serving

Instructions:

1. In a bowl, mix tuna, sriracha, sesame oil, and mayonnaise. Set aside.
2. Lay the nori on a bamboo mat, shiny side down.
3. Spread a thin layer of sushi rice over the nori, leaving a 1-inch edge at the top.
4. Add a line of spicy tuna mixture and optional cucumber or avocado slices.
5. Roll tightly using the bamboo mat, sealing the edge with a bit of water.
6. Slice into 6-8 pieces using a sharp knife.
7. Serve with soy sauce, pickled ginger, and wasabi.

Matcha Green Tea Ice Cream

Ingredients:

- 1 cup whole milk
- 2 cups heavy cream
- 3/4 cup sugar
- 2 tbsp matcha green tea powder
- 4 egg yolks

Instructions:

1. In a saucepan, heat milk and sugar over medium heat until sugar dissolves.
2. Whisk egg yolks in a bowl, then slowly pour the hot milk into the yolks while whisking.
3. Return the mixture to the pan and cook on low heat, stirring constantly, until thickened.
4. Dissolve matcha powder in a small amount of warm water, then stir into the custard.
5. Chill the mixture, then churn in an ice cream maker. Freeze until firm.

Classic Miso Soup

Ingredients:

- 4 cups dashi broth
- 3 tbsp miso paste
- 1/2 cup cubed tofu
- 2 tbsp wakame (dried seaweed)
- 2 green onions, sliced

Instructions:

1. Heat dashi in a pot but do not boil.
2. In a small bowl, dissolve miso paste with a ladleful of hot broth. Stir into the pot.
3. Add tofu and wakame. Simmer for 2-3 minutes.
4. Garnish with green onions and serve hot.

Pork Tonkatsu with Cabbage

Ingredients:

- 4 boneless pork chops
- 1 cup panko breadcrumbs
- 1/2 cup flour
- 2 eggs, beaten
- Salt and pepper
- Vegetable oil for frying
- Shredded cabbage for serving
- Tonkatsu sauce

Instructions:

1. Pound pork chops to 1/2-inch thickness. Season with salt and pepper.
2. Coat chops in flour, dip in eggs, then coat with panko.
3. Heat oil in a skillet and fry chops until golden and cooked through.
4. Serve with shredded cabbage and tonkatsu sauce.

Shrimp Tempura

Ingredients:

- 12 large shrimp, peeled and deveined
- 1 cup all-purpose flour
- 1 egg, lightly beaten
- 1 cup ice-cold water
- Oil for frying
- Tempura dipping sauce

Instructions:

1. Heat oil in a deep pan to 350°F (175°C).
2. Mix flour, egg, and cold water into a light batter. Do not overmix.
3. Dip shrimp into batter and fry until golden.
4. Drain on paper towels and serve with dipping sauce.

Japanese Curry Rice

Ingredients:

- 1 lb chicken or beef, cubed
- 1 onion, chopped
- 2 carrots, chopped
- 1 potato, cubed
- 4 cups water
- 1 package Japanese curry roux
- Steamed rice

Instructions:

1. Sauté meat and onions until browned.
2. Add carrots, potatoes, and water. Simmer until vegetables are tender.
3. Stir in curry roux until dissolved. Simmer until thickened.
4. Serve over steamed rice.

Yakitori Chicken Sticks

Ingredients:

- 1 lb chicken thighs, cut into bite-sized pieces
- Wooden skewers
- 1/4 cup soy sauce
- 2 tbsp mirin
- 2 tbsp sake
- 1 tbsp sugar

Instructions:

1. Mix soy sauce, mirin, sake, and sugar. Marinate chicken for 30 minutes.
2. Thread chicken onto skewers. Grill or broil, basting with marinade until cooked.

Okonomiyaki Savory Pancakes

Ingredients:

- 1 cup flour
- 2 eggs
- 2/3 cup dashi stock
- 2 cups shredded cabbage
- 1/4 cup chopped green onions
- Optional: sliced pork belly or shrimp
- Okonomiyaki sauce, mayonnaise, and bonito flakes for topping

Instructions:

1. Mix flour, eggs, and dashi to form a batter. Fold in cabbage and onions.
2. Pour batter into a hot oiled skillet, top with pork/shrimp, and cook until golden. Flip and cook the other side.
3. Drizzle with okonomiyaki sauce, mayonnaise, and top with bonito flakes.

Takoyaki Octopus Balls

Ingredients:

- 1 cup takoyaki batter mix
- 2 eggs
- 2 1/2 cups dashi stock
- Diced octopus, green onions, and pickled ginger
- Takoyaki sauce, mayonnaise, bonito flakes

Instructions:

1. Preheat takoyaki pan. Pour batter into greased molds.
2. Add octopus, green onions, and ginger to each mold.
3. Cook and rotate until golden and round.
4. Top with sauces and bonito flakes.

Salmon Onigiri (Rice Balls)

Ingredients:

- 2 cups cooked sushi rice
- 4 tbsp flaked cooked salmon
- Nori sheets
- Salt

Instructions:

1. Wet hands, sprinkle with salt, and shape rice into balls.
2. Add salmon to the center and reshape.
3. Wrap with a strip of nori.

Udon Noodle Stir-Fry

Ingredients:

- 8 oz udon noodles
- 1 cup sliced vegetables (e.g., bell peppers, carrots)
- 1/2 lb chicken or shrimp
- 2 tbsp soy sauce
- 1 tbsp oyster sauce
- 1 tsp sesame oil
- 2 cloves garlic, minced

Instructions:

1. Cook udon noodles and set aside.
2. Stir-fry garlic, vegetables, and protein in oil.
3. Add sauces and toss in noodles. Stir-fry until combined.

Mochi Desserts

Ingredients:

- 1 cup glutinous rice flour
- 3/4 cup water
- 1/4 cup sugar
- Cornstarch for dusting
- Optional filling: red bean paste or ice cream

Instructions:

1. Mix glutinous rice flour, water, and sugar in a microwave-safe bowl.
2. Microwave for 2 minutes, stir, then microwave for 1 more minute.
3. Dust a surface with cornstarch and knead the mochi until smooth.
4. Divide into portions, flatten, and wrap around the filling.

Japanese Cheesecake

Ingredients:

- 8 oz cream cheese, softened
- 1/4 cup milk
- 1/4 cup sugar
- 3 eggs, separated
- 1/4 cup flour
- 1/4 cup cornstarch
- 1/4 tsp cream of tartar

Instructions:

1. Preheat oven to 320°F (160°C). Line a springform pan with parchment.
2. Beat cream cheese, milk, and sugar until smooth. Add egg yolks, flour, and cornstarch.
3. Whip egg whites with cream of tartar until stiff peaks form, then fold into the batter.
4. Pour batter into the pan and bake in a water bath for 45-50 minutes. Cool before serving.

Wagyu Beef Steaks

Ingredients:

- 2 Wagyu beef steaks
- Salt and pepper
- 1 tbsp olive oil or butter

Instructions:

1. Bring steaks to room temperature and season with salt and pepper.
2. Heat oil or butter in a skillet over medium heat.
3. Sear steaks for 2-3 minutes on each side for medium-rare. Let rest before slicing.

Gyudon Beef Bowl

Ingredients:

- 1/2 lb thinly sliced beef
- 1/2 onion, thinly sliced
- 1/4 cup soy sauce
- 2 tbsp mirin
- 1 tbsp sugar
- 1 cup dashi stock
- Cooked rice

Instructions:

1. Sauté onion in a skillet until softened. Add dashi, soy sauce, mirin, and sugar.
2. Add beef and cook until tender.
3. Serve over rice, topped with green onions or a poached egg if desired.

Edamame with Sea Salt

Ingredients:

- 1 lb edamame in pods
- 1 tbsp sea salt

Instructions:

1. Boil edamame in salted water for 3-5 minutes.
2. Drain and sprinkle with sea salt. Serve warm or chilled.

Soy Glazed Eggplant

Ingredients:

- 2 medium eggplants, sliced
- 2 tbsp soy sauce
- 1 tbsp mirin
- 1 tbsp sugar
- 1 tsp sesame oil

Instructions:

1. Sear eggplant slices in sesame oil until tender.
2. Mix soy sauce, mirin, and sugar, then pour over eggplant.
3. Cook until the glaze thickens. Serve warm.

Gyoza Dumplings

Ingredients:

- 1 cup ground pork or chicken
- 1 cup chopped cabbage
- 2 green onions, minced
- 1 tbsp soy sauce
- 1 tsp sesame oil
- 1 package gyoza wrappers

Instructions:

1. Mix pork, cabbage, onions, soy sauce, and sesame oil.
2. Place a teaspoon of filling in a wrapper, moisten edges, and fold into a half-moon shape.
3. Pan-fry until bottoms are golden, then add water and cover to steam. Serve with dipping sauce.

Katsu Sando (Cutlet Sandwich)

Ingredients:

- 2 pork or chicken cutlets, breaded and fried (see Tonkatsu recipe)
- 4 slices Japanese milk bread
- Tonkatsu sauce
- Shredded cabbage

Instructions:

1. Spread tonkatsu sauce on bread slices.
2. Place cutlet and cabbage between slices.
3. Cut off crusts and slice into halves or thirds.

Cold Soba Noodle Salad

Ingredients:

- 8 oz soba noodles
- 1/4 cup soy sauce
- 2 tbsp mirin
- 1 tsp sesame oil
- Sliced cucumber, carrots, and green onions

Instructions:

1. Cook soba noodles according to package instructions, then rinse in cold water.
2. Mix soy sauce, mirin, and sesame oil. Toss with noodles and vegetables.
3. Serve chilled.

Tamago Sushi (Egg Sushi)

Ingredients:

- 2 eggs
- 1 tsp sugar
- 1/4 tsp soy sauce
- Cooked sushi rice
- Nori strips

Instructions:

1. Beat eggs with sugar and soy sauce. Cook in a thin layer in a non-stick pan. Fold into a rectangular shape.
2. Slice tamago into pieces, place on rice balls, and secure with nori strips.

Yakiniku Grilled Meats

Ingredients:

- 1 lb thinly sliced beef, pork, or chicken
- 1/4 cup soy sauce
- 2 tbsp mirin
- 1 tbsp sesame oil
- 1 tbsp sugar
- Grated garlic and ginger

Instructions:

1. Combine soy sauce, mirin, sesame oil, sugar, garlic, and ginger. Marinate meat for 30 minutes.
2. Grill or pan-fry meat over high heat until cooked.
3. Serve with rice and dipping sauces.

Hokkaido Butter Corn Ramen

Ingredients:

- 4 cups chicken broth
- 1 tbsp miso paste
- 2 tbsp butter
- 1/2 cup corn kernels
- 2 servings ramen noodles
- Sliced green onions, boiled egg, and nori for garnish

Instructions:

1. Heat broth and miso paste in a pot.
2. Cook ramen noodles separately.
3. Add butter and corn to the broth, stirring until butter melts.
4. Pour broth over noodles and top with garnishes.

Green Tea Mochi Cake

Ingredients:

- 1 cup glutinous rice flour
- 1/2 cup sugar
- 1 tbsp matcha powder
- 3/4 cup coconut milk
- 1/4 cup vegetable oil

Instructions:

1. Preheat oven to 350°F (175°C). Grease a small baking pan.
2. Mix all ingredients until smooth.
3. Pour batter into the pan and bake for 30-35 minutes.
4. Let cool before slicing.

Sweet Soy Dango Skewers

Ingredients:

- 1 cup glutinous rice flour
- 1/2 cup water
- 2 tbsp soy sauce
- 2 tbsp sugar
- 1 tbsp mirin

Instructions:

1. Mix rice flour and water to form a dough. Roll into small balls.
2. Boil dango until they float. Drain and cool.
3. Mix soy sauce, sugar, and mirin in a pan to make the glaze.
4. Skewer dango, brush with glaze, and grill briefly.

Tempura Zaru Soba

Ingredients:

- 8 oz soba noodles
- 1/2 cup tempura batter mix
- Water and ice
- Shrimp and vegetables (e.g., sweet potato, eggplant)
- Tempura dipping sauce

Instructions:

1. Cook soba noodles and rinse under cold water.
2. Mix tempura batter with ice-cold water. Dip shrimp and vegetables into batter and fry until golden.
3. Serve soba with dipping sauce and tempura on the side.

Sashimi Salad

Ingredients:

- 6 oz assorted sashimi (e.g., salmon, tuna)
- Mixed greens
- 2 tbsp soy sauce
- 1 tbsp rice vinegar
- 1 tbsp sesame oil
- 1 tsp grated ginger

Instructions:

1. Arrange sashimi and greens on a plate.
2. Mix soy sauce, vinegar, sesame oil, and ginger to make the dressing.
3. Drizzle dressing over the salad before serving.

Japanese Pickles (Tsukemono)

Ingredients:

- 1 cucumber, sliced
- 1/2 cup daikon radish, sliced
- 1 tbsp salt
- 1 tbsp sugar
- 2 tbsp rice vinegar

Instructions:

1. Sprinkle cucumber and daikon with salt. Let sit for 30 minutes. Rinse and drain.
2. Mix sugar and vinegar. Toss with vegetables.
3. Refrigerate for 1-2 hours before serving.

Shabu-Shabu Hot Pot

Ingredients:

- 1 lb thinly sliced beef or pork
- Napa cabbage, shiitake mushrooms, tofu, and udon noodles
- 6 cups dashi broth
- Ponzu or sesame dipping sauce

Instructions:

1. Heat dashi broth in a pot.
2. Place vegetables, tofu, and noodles in the broth.
3. Swish thin slices of meat in the hot broth until cooked. Dip into sauces before eating.

Chicken Karaage (Japanese Fried Chicken)

Ingredients:

- 1 lb chicken thighs, cut into bite-sized pieces
- 2 tbsp soy sauce
- 1 tbsp sake
- 1 tsp grated garlic
- 1 tsp grated ginger
- 1/2 cup potato starch
- Oil for frying

Instructions:

1. Marinate chicken in soy sauce, sake, garlic, and ginger for 20 minutes.
2. Coat chicken with potato starch.
3. Deep-fry until golden and crispy. Drain on paper towels before serving.

Seaweed Salad

Ingredients:

- 1 cup dried seaweed mix, rehydrated
- 2 tbsp soy sauce
- 1 tbsp rice vinegar
- 1 tsp sesame oil
- Sesame seeds for garnish

Instructions:

1. Rehydrate seaweed in water and drain.
2. Mix soy sauce, vinegar, and sesame oil. Toss with seaweed.
3. Sprinkle with sesame seeds before serving.

Chawanmushi (Savory Egg Custard)

Ingredients:

- 2 large eggs
- 1 cup dashi broth
- 1 tsp soy sauce
- 1 tsp mirin
- Fillings (e.g., shrimp, chicken, mushrooms)

Instructions:

1. Whisk eggs, dashi, soy sauce, and mirin until smooth. Strain to remove bubbles.
2. Place fillings in cups, pour egg mixture over.
3. Steam on low heat for 10-15 minutes, covered with foil, until set.

Japanese Fried Rice (Chahan)

Ingredients:

- 2 cups cooked rice
- 1/2 cup diced vegetables (carrot, peas, etc.)
- 2 eggs, beaten
- 1/4 cup diced ham or shrimp
- 1 tbsp soy sauce
- 1 tbsp sesame oil

Instructions:

1. Heat sesame oil in a wok, scramble eggs, and set aside.
2. Sauté vegetables and ham/shrimp. Add rice and mix well.
3. Add soy sauce, stir in scrambled eggs, and cook until heated through.

Mackerel Sushi (Saba)

Ingredients:

- 2 fillets of mackerel
- 1 cup sushi rice, cooked
- 1/4 cup rice vinegar
- 1 tbsp sugar
- 1 tsp salt

Instructions:

1. Mix vinegar, sugar, and salt into warm rice.
2. Cure mackerel by sprinkling salt, letting it sit for 15 minutes, then rinsing and soaking in vinegar for 20 minutes.
3. Lay cured mackerel over a bed of sushi rice and press into a mold. Slice before serving.

Spicy Mayo Shrimp Rolls

Ingredients:

- 1 cup cooked shrimp, chopped
- 2 tbsp mayonnaise
- 1 tsp sriracha
- Nori sheets
- 1 cup sushi rice, cooked
- Sliced avocado and cucumber

Instructions:

1. Mix shrimp, mayo, and sriracha.
2. Spread rice over nori, place avocado, cucumber, and shrimp mix in the center.
3. Roll tightly, slice, and serve with soy sauce.

Matcha Latte

Ingredients:

- 1 tsp matcha powder
- 1/4 cup hot water
- 3/4 cup steamed milk
- 1 tsp sugar or honey (optional)

Instructions:

1. Whisk matcha powder and hot water until smooth.
2. Add steamed milk and sweetener if desired. Serve warm.

Eel Donburi (Unadon)

Ingredients:

- 2 grilled eel fillets (unagi)
- 2 cups cooked rice
- 1/4 cup soy sauce
- 2 tbsp mirin
- 1 tbsp sugar

Instructions:

1. Heat soy sauce, mirin, and sugar in a pan to make a glaze.
2. Brush eel with glaze and broil until caramelized.
3. Serve over rice with extra glaze drizzled on top.

Japanese Potato Salad

Ingredients:

- 2 potatoes, boiled and mashed
- 1/4 cup diced cucumber
- 1/4 cup diced carrots, boiled
- 2 tbsp mayonnaise
- Salt and pepper to taste

Instructions:

1. Mix mashed potatoes with cucumbers, carrots, and mayonnaise.
2. Season with salt and pepper. Chill before serving.

Tuna Tataki

Ingredients:

- 1 tuna steak
- 1 tbsp soy sauce
- 1 tbsp rice vinegar
- 1 tsp sesame oil
- Sesame seeds for coating

Instructions:

1. Coat tuna with sesame seeds. Sear for 20 seconds on each side in sesame oil.
2. Slice thinly and drizzle with soy sauce and rice vinegar.

Kabocha Tempura

Ingredients:

- 1/2 kabocha squash, sliced thinly
- 1/2 cup tempura batter mix
- Ice-cold water
- Oil for frying

Instructions:

1. Mix tempura batter with ice-cold water.
2. Dip kabocha slices in the batter and fry until golden.
3. Serve with tempura dipping sauce.

Japanese Sweet Red Bean Soup (Zenzai)

Ingredients:

- 1 cup red azuki beans
- 1/2 cup sugar
- 4 cups water
- 4 pieces of mochi (store-bought or homemade)

Instructions:

1. Soak azuki beans in water for several hours, then drain.
2. Boil beans in fresh water for 10 minutes, then drain again.
3. Add 4 cups of water and boil beans until tender.
4. Stir in sugar and simmer until slightly thickened.
5. Toast or grill mochi, then serve in the soup.

Sukiyaki Beef Hotpot

Ingredients:

- 1/2 lb thinly sliced beef
- 1/2 block tofu, cubed
- 1 cup Napa cabbage, chopped
- 1/2 cup sliced shiitake mushrooms
- 1/4 cup soy sauce
- 1/4 cup mirin
- 2 tbsp sugar
- 1/4 cup dashi broth

Instructions:

1. Combine soy sauce, mirin, sugar, and dashi in a pot. Bring to a simmer.
2. Add vegetables, tofu, and beef, cooking in layers.
3. Simmer until cooked through. Serve with rice or a raw egg dipping sauce.

Yuzu Sorbet

Ingredients:

- 1 cup yuzu juice
- 1/2 cup sugar
- 1 cup water

Instructions:

1. Heat water and sugar until dissolved. Let cool.
2. Mix yuzu juice with syrup and chill.
3. Churn in an ice cream maker or freeze, stirring every hour, until firm.

Japanese Street Crepes

Ingredients:

- 1 cup all-purpose flour
- 1 tbsp sugar
- 2 eggs
- 1 cup milk
- Butter for greasing
- Fillings (e.g., whipped cream, fruit, chocolate syrup, red bean paste)

Instructions:

1. Whisk flour, sugar, eggs, and milk until smooth. Let batter rest for 30 minutes.
2. Heat a nonstick pan, grease with butter, and cook thin crepes.
3. Fill with desired ingredients and fold into cones.

Nikujaga (Meat and Potato Stew)

Ingredients:

- 1/2 lb sliced beef or pork
- 2 potatoes, peeled and diced
- 1/2 onion, sliced
- 2 cups dashi broth
- 2 tbsp soy sauce
- 1 tbsp sugar
- 1 tbsp mirin

Instructions:

1. Sauté meat and onions until lightly browned.
2. Add potatoes and dashi broth. Simmer for 10 minutes.
3. Stir in soy sauce, sugar, and mirin. Cook until potatoes are tender.

Shio Ramen

Ingredients:

- 4 cups chicken broth
- 1 tsp salt
- 1 tsp soy sauce
- 1/2 tsp sesame oil
- Ramen noodles
- Toppings (e.g., soft-boiled egg, nori, green onions, chicken slices)

Instructions:

1. Heat chicken broth and season with salt, soy sauce, and sesame oil.
2. Cook ramen noodles separately.
3. Pour broth over noodles and add toppings.

Chirashi Sushi Bowl

Ingredients:

- 1 cup sushi rice, cooked
- 1/4 cup rice vinegar
- Assorted sashimi (e.g., tuna, salmon, shrimp)
- Sliced cucumber, shredded nori, and pickled ginger for garnish

Instructions:

1. Mix rice vinegar into warm rice.
2. Arrange rice in a bowl, top with sashimi and garnishes.

Daifuku Mochi with Strawberry

Ingredients:

- 1 cup glutinous rice flour
- 1/2 cup sugar
- 3/4 cup water

- Red bean paste
- 6 strawberries

Instructions:

1. Mix rice flour, sugar, and water. Microwave for 2 minutes, stir, then microwave for another minute until sticky.
2. Dust hands with cornstarch, flatten dough, and wrap around a strawberry with red bean paste.
3. Shape into balls and let cool.

www.ingramcontent.com/pod-product-compliance
Lightning Source LLC
LaVergne TN
LVHW081337060526
838201LV00055B/2710